COMMANDO

E'mon Lauren

D1399443

© 2017 E'mon Lauren

Published in 2017 by
Haymarket Books
P.O. Box 180165
Chicago, IL 60618
www.haymarketbooks.org

ISBN: 978-1-60846-943-7

Trade distribution:
In the US, Consortium Book Sales and Distribution, www.cbsd.com
In Canada, Publishers Group Canada, www.pgcbooks.ca
In the UK, Turnaround Publisher Services, www.turnaround-uk.com
All other countries, Ingram Publisher Services International,
IPS_Intlsales@ingramcontent.com

This book was published with the generous support of Lannan Foundation
and Wallace Action Fund.

Cover art by Bianca Pastel.

Entered into digital printing September, 2017.

For me.
For baby.
For Ma Dukes and Daddy.
For the body.
For the fighting.
For the sightings.
For the bodies.
For the hood hobbies.
For the hood lobby.
For the Englewood droppings.
For L Town likings.
For the shooters/hittas/brothas/sistas/movas/drillas/ protecting.
For the block blessing.

"I'm only nineteen, but my mind is old.
And when the things get for real, my warm heart turns cold."

—Prodigy of Mobb Deep (Shook Ones PT 2), 1995

Speak

i got a family reunion in my mouth. chuuch under my tongue. loud
packed loose squared language. bootlegged babble. mild saucy and
slick. quick card crackin gramma. squad a sanctuary on my top lip.
throw the handles of my cheeks. what's good in the hood of your
mouth? the yo in my yawn. a fugase flap/flick of tongue. southside
schtick slobbered. a candy lady's cabinet. bud and MC lite/Lyte a
boombox on my beak. suited and booted. food and liquor leaking.
tripping on my tonsil. a(1/k47). the rink skating on my *no*'s and
what consent mean. my gots belong to Giovanni and Jasmine. a
different world in a dutch masters. elbows off the table of my teeth.
don't you have any manners. melanin in the suck. Auntie Pokie neck
roll caught in my throat. i speak a queer language. color coded. no
code switch or swap in my mouth. i hold a rainbow coalition on my
tongue. obama care in my back throat. let my Mom claim the baby
in my teeth for tax season. i speak sacrifice. urban dictionary in the
suburbs. know my rights and speak them. loud. like my music. like
my body. like my bossy. i speak my bossy. i speak Trina and Cardi B.
i speak womyn runs the house. i speak field and house. i speak house.
chicago. chicagu. chic-a-go. redline lingering lick. i speak shaa(r)p.
sharp sword. bible translations. revenue. avenues and blvds. stomping
grounds when i chew. cabrini mouths Moms greens. leclaire courts
on 26th and california. i speak free my mans. i speak free my energy.
i speak in royalist. in concrete king/queendoms.

Mary Lou

lived in the biggest house on the block
     in l town
      at north ave & leclaire
the biggest house made for 2 families
                that fit 8.
the biggest house on the street
that never got robbed
         on christmas.

the candy lady for all
the leslie lewis elementary kids
even the ones who wouldn't let me sit at their lunch table
even the ones who would.
the best nacho maker on the block
used two different doritos
convinced Nikki they're better than her dad's tacos
convinced Nikki food was safe
even from people darker than her
even from people who ain't her.

the kitchen a hair shop
on easter and passover
working on mines,
and Aiyanna's
and Ashley's
and Jada's
and Gabrielle's
and Snookie's
and steve's baby's
even the babies he never claimed
even the baby mamas who claim they got him on child support

even my sister who never put him on child support
even my sister who is still a child with 4 children.

the nanny on the 1st and 15th
the finesser of a 5 dollar handshake
10 on my birthday
20   with good grades
30   just because it was her last
                    from the bills
1 dollar even if it was   her last.

My Cousin Called Those Redbone Girls 'Milli Vanillies'

the milli vanillies are the shorties i learned to fight. the ones that jumped me at rainey. the ones that taught me to juke. the ones that took me to markham. put me on with they ex. fought me after. fucked my mans. who mans still text me. the ones i go to clinics with. watch baby boy with. the ones who lie for love. lie for a bed. lie for a meal. the ones who lye. who screenshot. subtweet. call private. the ones who leave they momma crib. the ones who moms don't have a crib. the ones who find a mom in other's. who open everybody fridge. who need the wifi code. who take the hoodies. who never give them back. the ones determined to take. the ones looking for whatever was taken from them. who carry vaseline like a baby. gives theirs like a closed fist. the ones hacking his page. the ones who use windows as shadows. run away from theirs. used as ground. in search of a foundation. build their church in the home of whatever body they have left. the prey of another man's prayer. the ones that found their god. the ones who hopes he comes home. the ones unsure of what he's coming home too. the ones unsure of which house he will go to. the ones who know. the lie. the ones who know. the truth. the ones who are lying to
themselves
like me.

Chic-a-go

where a chic-a-go blow
in the wind for a cluck
for uncle harold and all
his saucy manners dressed
in the mildest ways. stay respecting
the spiciness. spiced up
slight cuts/coldest
cuts from the pack/ back
of the trains. back
handed a train/been trained
know it well in all
our hot sauce. hop
throwing hips/twinkle toed
skyline rhythm:
a beat mixed/taped hot
dopest/harvest. kool-aid
ices mixing/maxwell dogs. a new
stomach to sit on. chic-a-go's
go make that money
for the fams/frans
squads on t shirts. repping
their 10th family
reunion/repping all
jojo's on the block. repping
all the time.
simeon and morgan park
annual championship basketball game
fast in all lanes.
rush hour home
panda express for bae
play some chance and ye

rap our hearts blue
til the light turn/ignition
red,
or yellow/we rarely slow down for
speed up. the air is too thin
to breathe/ we stay on key.
hold our lungs in sacrifice
to god/we pray
the sun shines a little
harder. when the calendar says
it's suppose to. never go that way;
3 season past due/winters last till june.
southside heat/be blossoming into story
books and burning dreams
chic-a-go be burning leaves.
got sage/sane for the freshly woke.
more air for the toke/pull of cloves.
4 lucky stars/a quartered yard
shares 8 veins/trains.
minding the mildest
ways.

79th Be The Catwalk.

Tyra Banks ain't got shit,
taxes just hit. folks
strut. here is the timber
of our land. we give
the breeze a new cover. girl
some dude with a camera said he could
buy my walk, plus interest
my face. ain't enough
to want my body too. move
like i got somewhere to be. round
here home ain't much of america's
model. my landlord
said i walk like money,
a stain/finesse. examination
is extermination. what was
a short cut is now a safe word
kept for cutting. or just in case
some fool thinks a south side stomp
sweet. commercial. commissary is
a blk girl's stride. to the bus
be blk boiis who grab
their dickies. gucci belt gang
expect me to hold they strap. loose
square sellers all off theirs,
ready to lick or hit one.
they think the bus'll wait for me
but someone else ready to take my spot.
like the white man's hunt ain't my job too. like
they ain't got somewhere to be too. like
we ain't in hurry to go
someplace where we can just walk.

The Etymology of "CHUUCH!"

chuuch/church

[pronounced without the "r". the "r" is the hump on our backs. too much to weigh/wait.
imagine replacing the "r" with "u". the cupping is softer. all the things it holds. it often sounds like "ahh". round and complete. it all comes together. like home.]

1. from the renowned *amen*. meaning *let it be*. or *so it is*. or so may have it. and take into agreement. this the stamp. the let it be said and sold. the solidarity screaming from the stem of our spouts. this is the *yes*.

2. used in positions of *incognegro*. the screech beyond the never lands of our blocks. posted and protecting. remember the code. often known as *i peep game*. or the never ending *i'm on it bro*. closing the deal. the celebration of *i see you*. welcome to my memory for another day. let the house of our bodies be be grateful. for our sacrifices has not killed us. yet.

3. said like a vaccine. the awkwardness dancing on your lip before your words fall and ruin the show. this can also be the broken promise. the text you know you won't reply to. the person you drag your heart for with no supplies left to clean. this is sometimes the last stake. the call of *i don't understand, but imma figure this shit out*. the choir is singing and you can't understand anything sang. so you sing. for the house is still bouncing. ace boom cooling.

4. this is not to be confused with *sending off*. it's the most honest thing we are unsure of. for every house is not covered. we cover our prayer with a *this is it*. *this is real* and our lives. we do not *agree* to this condition of our wellbeing. blast and break our cinderblocks like tambourines. we weave the

stories together. thank and talk through our teeth. for *we
know. we understand.* we light the sky. shake up with god
and find the move. keep the key. keep it pushing.

The Etymology of a Blk Girl's Name or Being Tongue Tied During Sex

a blk girls name is meant to be
said like a drunk night. swishing
and gargled around a bar stool.

a blk girls name
is pronounced like a loiter/labor/later
in the alley, your mother left
open. niggas think they can speak
my syllables. say my names is *yes* enough
then stumble when it don't stick
the first time. i gave someone my name
and was later a butcher shop.
men take the meek for meat and forget
the name of the meal.

a blk girls name is to be said like sex
talk. tongue tied. between birth
certificate and ball point pen.

Last Name

not blade brown but blade   Black
house party pitch   Black
juke basement and dirty ones   Black
one shade not 50   Black
21 questions   Black
ask the right way   Black
use your manners   Black
mother may i?   Black
Ms. Mary used to babysit   Black
Moms at the bar   Black
bought/buy her/you a drank   Black
a few of em   Black
keep em coming   Black
killed the family   Black
resting on the rocks   Black
cold as ice   Black
say fuck everybody   Black
need none/nobody   Black
even if the lights out   Black
got a new pitch   Black
jehovah's witness   Black
slam doors/hard headed   Black
brain aneurysms   Black
granddad   Black
revolver in the mouth   **Black**
Auntie Pokie caught him   **Black**
can't keep secrets   **Black**
got too many   **Black**

Micros and Aggression

yeah nigga. i make cereal from cornbread. got a box fan year round.
don't sweat it. i like my hair remy wet. my hair is mines with or
without receipt. the beauty supply is a doll house. yeah i had barbies.
burnt them bitches to look like me. taught them how to talk too. they
knew every -er turn to an -a. knew every 'finna' came from 'fix-in'. i
fixed them. glamorized their thick or thin like mines was. yeah nigga.
i'm thick. my ass always gone poke. like you did and do. on facebook.
on the bus. on the train. in the store. in the house. in my house. like
it never happened. like it was an accident. call it educational. call it a
means of survival. my Moms calls it means for an ass-whooping. calls
it switch blade and sets of keys. calls it protection. you call it an-
gry-blk-woman. tyler perry movies on repeat. i call it a never ending
novel. fuck the single story. Chimamanda taught me. yeah nigga. i
twerk for scholarships or just because. had my homie crack my card
for bail money. wrote a thesis on why you got me fucked up. earned
commission on the hands you can catch but can't hold.

Ode to Saggy Titties

two roads diverged/ over my brown
hood/pudding escaping
form and hold/ fat falling off of
cliffs/ natural disasters/ hot
milk in tea bags/
my ribcage compass/ the sun rises over
my lopsided hills/ east and west twins/
leaning towers of melanin/ bricks
melting in heat/ the storage spaces
of my heart/ stretched out
and free

Ode to Eczema

melanin patched and parted/
itch kissing cuticle/ rough
rugs of flesh/ a camel's back
all over my body/ a mahogany
monet/ my skin
/rid me of rash/ fingertips
tap dancing in overtime/
raking dead brown/ turned
white and flake/ floating
cinnamon specks/
brown body fading
a colored lottery ticket/
stitched by allergy/ a resewn
reaction / self-made quilt

Ode to Pubes

lover. there was a rug made
for my house of holes. after you've felt
all warmth, you take home
in shaven sanctuary. and i
prick and ponder
over my rugless house. is love
building my home from scratch?
between my thick sky,
you hunt.
pluck your findings before you feast
and return home.
you find warmth and think
me home. for you
it's dry air to breathe. after
i remove my rugs.
because you've kept yours. only
for me to be bare
and cold and growing.

A Window-Shopping-Ass-Nigga

after Morgan Parker's "Matt"

always a send a pic ass nigga, a netflix and chill ass nigga even
though he ain't got no x-box, just pawned it for a tre-five, said he
was gone flip it, always being a flip-flop, sturdy as a pair of flip-flops,
singing about some gucci flip-flops knowing damn well you win-
dow-shop at gucci, water tower ass niggas, window seat at mcdon-
ald's cuz they got outlets ass niggas, hit the chick-fil-a 10 minutes
later for they wifi ass niggas, ask for a courtesy cup and fill it with
all the pops, spend his last dollar on a black & mild, now he gotta
try to finesse the bus driver, knew the bus driver wasn't going in the
first place, always testing the waters, jesus walking in a food desert,
thirsty like vultures, a "wassup gorgeous" ass nigga, a "lemme take
you out" when i just saw you stain two honey-buns ass nigga, loose
squares ass nigga asking me for a lighter; always ready to play a game
with no pieces, boards been broken before they bought it, wonder
why i'on give you no play, wonder why i only do on tuesdays, wonder
why i'on invite you to shows, wonder why i gave you my old number,
never thought to check if it was working in the first place, always
be the first to tell me they resume without me having to ask, really
hope he actually got a resume, know he could be a good hood ass
nigga, know he prolly came from the good side of the hood, know
he prolly jumping wrong-sided tracks, said he gone always see green
on the other side, call it sawbucks and quarters ass niggas, outside
looking in ass niggas, always being watched ass niggas, got a being as
a window ass niggas, wonder why i won't let you in, wonder why my
door stays bolted, tired of hearing my ex's story ass niggas, promise
he'll protect me ass niggas, told him my ex said the same thing, came
through my window and beat my ass nigga, guess i was to transpar-
ent, called it committment, now it's just robbery ass niggas, always
ready to take ass niggas, never wanting to buy ass niggas, wanna

know where the clearance rack is, told him i don't have one, still
breaking windows, drink windex like whiskey, don't care about the
merchandise, just wanna stand in front of the store
                                        and never buy shit.

(Re)cycle

mr. airforce guy is a dude who been hurt.
i told mr. airforce guy i was a good girl
for him. but i'm tryna figure this
shit out cuz mfs still hurting me.

i got this other dude,
the artist. he is tooo sweet,
gives me all that shit
i be asking for without ever having to
give my body.
don't even gotta open my mouth (much)
but i'm doing him bogus too.
cuz he hella good and i'm low key
that bitch that's sneaking.
only a little bit tho.
only for my protection
tho. i promise,
but funny thing is,
now i'm that bitch that done hurt mr. airforce guy.
but he ain't acting right still
so fuck it.

this is the reason i keep niggas
on hiatus. cuz mfs take you through the notions
and shit. got you feeling all special and important
like yo momma rightfully claimed yo birth to be,
beautiful or a fucking
blessing for some man to call me/my phone number.
but nah.
here i am still.
one nigga already right

no acting needed,
and the other doing too much.

Sanctuary of Heathens

my room has been smelling
like paris. my legs turn everything
into an ash
and potential prayer/praise dance
or day.
hallowed be thy name
like this bottle of moscato; breaking
between my ankles. my shoe size
stomped the water out my bed.
floated home found my passport
under the porch. waiting
for me, to stamp the story.
holy shower myself.

the viaduct that's on ada st.
is wilting. looks
like it's dancing, on some
real jazz shit. fuck that
french. voulez-vous coucher
coochie voodoo.
i'm frisky/flimsy/freaky.
us females/bitches/pussy/kats/kool woos/womyn
call them bae/windows
and baby groove. grip and grind
our grunts for you

men: bow
and say it ain't clean enough.
say it's to dry for innocence. this
ain't no flint mission. move
like the lake. i'm tired

of these travelers, trippin'
these foreigners.
flippin' their blood through my hips, then don't
understand why the land is so barren.
don't bring your mess
no. blessings. i have
no more water to clean
my face from your mourning/breath.

Preamble

for Jessica Hampton

we the side bitches/pieces
of this union
in order to find a more profitable nigga
get a nut off
and catch the 6 like a run in our tights.
to ensure that we are as clean as the shower before.
domestic abuse is not a catalyst for a dm slide
a read receipt turned off
the morning he wakes up more american macho.

this is the for the people
flushed down the toilet like a carton of angels.

~~dearly beloved~~

we the side bitches/pieces of
this red line system
in order to tell him my results
trust the taken seat next to me
and still die before my blood has set its alarm
or his.
to ensure this breathing pillow is a sacrifice
a contingency prayer
a 47th street stabbing in the basement of my headboard.

i the side bitch/piece of his underwear drawer
whom he holds onto like a single ride ticket
or a platform argument he has already lost.

The Womb's Prayer

give me today a pregnancy test
help me to piss and stress straight
tho i walk through the valley of planned parenthood
i shall fear no sterile weapon or spermicide
hallowed be thy name and now body
barren make me a broken magic trick
abracadabra acrobat with a 8:30 appointment
now she here
now she sedated
heavenly father who ain't mine or my child's
make me a murderer and mother all at once
forgive my sin and flourish
for i am here
and i am blk
and my blood has stopped

heavenly father who give
i've made a blk child and a possible indictment
may the sheeps on these walls keep these thick thighs narrowed
may today be not another body lost

                    but saved

Mother's Day?

who gives me flowers
who made a grave
who robbed the cradle
who stole the day
who made today happy
who calls this spring
who celebrates the sickness
who celebrates the choices
who celebrates the plans
who celebrates the steps
who celebrates the here now
who celebrates the half that isn't
who makes womyn a buried building
who gives a sonogram an elegy
who marks a date with nothing due
who owes herself
who makes a funeral before the birth
who holds the morning hair
who makes a pillow more body than person
who sees theirs in everyone else's
who eats alone
who picks the window seat
who is still a grandmother
who hopes for redo's
who thinks today is still
who thinks today is still for them
who thinks today is still for them to call their own
who thinks today is a prayer
who made today trading places
who made me a growing belly
who made me a gargling fume

who made me the morning after
who made me the next day
who made my world a crashing idea
who made it a lost one

Dialogue

WHAT YOU MEAN NO. MINES. MILES AND MIND.
MILD. FEED AND FREAK YOU RIGHT AND YOU SAY NO.
GO. GREEN AND GROWING A LAND FOR ME. MEAT.
FRESH FEAST OF THE HUNT. BATTLE CRY AFTER THE
WAR. PAINT. YOUR INSIDES CLAD. CLASSY AND CRISP.
OUR SHEETS. YOUR ENTOMBING. ENTER AS I PLEASE.
I'VE GIVEN. EXITS. DRIVES. DIVES. DIPS. DIS. DAT.
DATES. DAMN. BE DAMNED TO BE A FOOL. FOOD. FEED
ME. BEASTLY. BEATING. BE THE BEST. BE THE BEAM.
ULTRA LIGHT. I'M LIGHTING. ADONIS FOR YOUR ASH-
ES. FEEL THE BURN. FEEL THE BURDEN. I'M BURROW-
ING. YOU ARE MY CUDDLE NET. MY WISP AND WASP.
WASHED DOWN IN MY WEB. YOU ARE SOLO. SULTRY
AND WRINKLED SILK. AND I AM PRESSED. AND I WILL
KEEP PRESSING. UNTIL THE PRESSURE IS PURE. AND
POWER IS MY PALM FULL. YA KNOW?

//.

color me core.
desert the sweet
between my thighs.
red velvet vixen .
flipped five fold.
fabricate the gold
of my Daughters edges.
the horizon over her head.
my Mother's a maker.
she is the poem.
a lumberjack birthing.
been broke/barren/blk.

burnt her back. tryna fly.
escape the bottle.
purify the puff.
pass our purpose in pads.
womyn are water.
i pity your position.
your love a picture. i'll pass
on your puzzle. Moms left me
all the books my closet could fill.
i feel like a fistful.
i am not your morning coffee.
tea to sip. i'm your secret
fear. your best exposure.
the whole
damn frame.

Blk Ars

after Krista Franklin, Jamila Woods

poems aint shit without the hood   rat studded belt and basement
   i'm going down after   eleven years wrote   choked/chalked all the
outline of myself   no more games   can't hop skip away
won't stop   jeff chang for change   spare some they don't
   really care about us   beat it   ms jean said come   home she
ain't my momma put vicks in the nose   a hot towel on your back
something   you aint use too   it   ain't shit if it don't
feel   like a scare you still give   to your partner mother   may i
permission needed   red light mean go   green   bucket
boy   blasting baby phat sagging apple bottom ace   boom cooling
convent and   convenient push ya cap back blue don't touch
me homie   you don't know me/my name   i don't want no
scrub poems   aint shit without   the vaccine 10 stitches and a
switch why you crying   we ain't got mcdonald's money   like
forreal   art stuff   hold you down   run it   pon de replay   poems
be the 9 mm   on a thick hip rip   meter run off and leave
meters running   nothing is   free not even   the parking

Commando Manifesto

***to be completely bare, openness can be a form of protection too
chicago, the block and the hood - environment controlled by masculinity
a lot of times as womyn we use our bareness, vulnerability to survive
we use our bodies, hearts on our arms to survive and be who the fuck we
are***

i wear my heart on my sleeves
i don't wear them much
chicago rips them right off of ya
so i like to get naked
now i'm a chested tube top
left my shoulders of skyscrapers open
ready for a kiss
ready for a blow
a job i can finish

Mom calls me a clever girl
said i would figure it out
taught me how to get out and be open
so i strip
gave niggas/men what they been asking for
kept plenty of blade in my tongue
might have knees that make pain or take it away
i learned my place and made it a throne
i fuck royally
turned my bed into a mauseoleum of offerings
my body is a sacrifice of my winnings
my trophies out in the open
who the fuck should i lay bare other than myself

i choose
to be commando
ready for action
ready to fight
for my land is mine
and it's still rich
and still ours
me
and whoever i choose to be
with
for whatever reason
some call it a weak move
a vulnerable ventra card
a roadmap of all my soft spots

here is where i plant my flag
might've be a pitstop for niggas who needed a home too
chicago's bosom been sagging on them for a while now
so i give mine
cook some meals
roll some blunts and fuck for free
cuz that love shit costs nowadays
ain't much here up for profit anyway
but people find a way
use my name
try to turn me into gentrified zone
throw some good words around me
add a splash of color
give me a stage and say work
bitch

i add the work
bitch
some crack music
some real blk ruthless

grind my pretty and talk real well
deposit my dialects
spit shine the ground i walk on
for this is mines
and no one can take me

Thanks/Gratitude

TO ALMIGHTY JEHOVAH FIRST OF ALL!

To Young Chicago Authors. To Anna Festa, Rebecca Hunter, Heather "Byrd" Roberts, Mariah, Tammy, and all. For making this the home that no one can take away. For being the family, friends, mentors, and crew. Thank you for the work.

To Kuumba Lynx Performance Ensemble. To Jacinda, Jaquanda and Maddog. The fight. The fist to pen. The stage, the poem, the body. All one in movement.

To Haymarket for publishing my first set of poems.

To the editors and friends who made this a never ending process.

To Urban Word NYC and Young Chicago Authors for awarding me the title of Chicago's first Youth Poet Laureate.

To ma: Laura L. Black Kelly. Thank you for the pen. The passion. For making me the greatest story you ever told. For never letting me tell myself "no". For teaching me "can't" is "complacent". For loving me in all fuckups and life-line attempts. For being the matriarch.

To daddy: Danny L. McGee. For loving me in spirit and all above. For keeping me exactly where I need to be. Rest in Poetry my father.

To the blood I hold onto: Aiyanna, Ashley, Jada, Gabrielle.

To my sistas: Sakeenah, Jamila, Cierra, Kamaria, and Ebony.

To my brethren: Andre "Drehunna", Keith "ChiBlu" and Trel.
HUEYGang: Mani Jurdan, Lockwood, DJ Cymba, Law, Stark,
KATO, and the whole set. Thank you for keeping your sister safe
and "unfuckwitable".

To my forever mentors turned forever family: Uncle Kevin Coval,
Jamila Woods, Nate Marshall, my double OG: Britteney Black Rose
Kapri, Fatimah Asghar, Adam Levin, and Avery R. Young. Thank
you for opening homes, doors, books and pages.

To my crew for keeping me grounded in the work: Toaster, Britteney,
Blu, my OG/twin sister Kush Thompson, and Matt Muse. Thank
you for making my job a blessing.

To the poetry gawwds I look up too: Morgan Parker, Jamila Woods,
Patricia Smith, Danez Smith, Mahogany L. Browne, Safia Elhillo,
Krista Franklin, Angel Nafis, Fatimah Asghar, Idris Goodwin, Nora
Brooks, Angela Jackson, Kevin Coval, Nate Marshall, Rita Dove,
Lucille Clifton, Marcus Jackson, Amiri Baraka, Mama Gwendolyn,
Nikki Giovanni, Phillis Wheatley and many more before me. For
giving me so much lineage to write after.

To my folks, squads, gangs, set of associates, homies, brethren, sistas,
healers, and believers. The ones that keep me going. Thank you
Sammy, Patricia, Kara, Jalen, Sara, Naudia, Antwon, Subi, Melinda.
For keeping the work engraved.

Rest in Power: Auntie Pokie (04/12 - 06/18/16)

E'MON LAUREN

is from the South Side of Chicago. She is a Scorpio enthusiast and a firm believer in Dorthy Dandridge reincarnation. E'mon uses poetry and playwriting to explore a philosophy of hood womanism. She was named Chicago's first Youth Poet Laureate. A former Kuumba Lynx Performance Ensemble slam team member and Louder Than a Bomb champion, E'mon has performed in many venues including The Brave New Voices International Youth Poetry Festival and The Chicago Hip Hop Theatre Fest. She was a 2016 finalist for The Gwendolyn Brooks Open Mic Award. E'mon has been published in *The BreakBeat Poets: New American Poetry in the Age of Hip-Hop*, *The Down Dirty Word*, and elsewhere. She has been featured in *Chicago Magazine*, the *Chicago Tribune*, and on WGN Radio. She is a member of Young Chicago Authors Teaching Artist Corps.

CPSIA information can be obtained
at www.ICGtesting.com
Printed in the USA
LVOW10s1658271117
557086LV00013B/14/P

9 781608 469437